I WITNESS WAR

THE WAR IN AFGHANISTAN

CLAUDIA MARTIN

Cavendish
Square

New York

Published in 2018 by Cavendish Square Publishing, LLC
243 5th Avenue, Suite 136, New York, NY 10016

Cataloging-in-Publication Data

Names: Martin, Claudia.
Title: The war in Afghanistan / Claudia Martin.
Description: New York : Cavendish Square, 2018. | Series: I witness war | Includes glossary and index. | Audience: Grades 5–8.
Identifiers: ISBN 9781502632623 (library bound) | ISBN 9781502634375 (pbk.) | ISBN 9781502632616 (ebook)
Subjects: LCSH: Afghan War, 2001-—Juvenile literature.
Classification: LCC DS371.412 M338 2018 | DDC 958.104'7—dc23

Produced for Cavendish Square by Calcium
Editors: Sarah Eason and Jennifer Sanderson
Designers: Paul Myerscough and Simon Borrough
Picture Researcher: Rachel Blount

Picture credits: Cover: DVIDS: US Army photo by Capt. Jarrod Morris; Inside: Shutterstock: Usoltceva Anastasiia 43, Anthony Correia 9, Nate Derrick 5, Peter Hermes Furian 4, Knovakov 15, Maximum Exposure PR 19, Northfoto 1, 7, Lizette Potgieter 8, Carolina K. Smith MD 30; Wikimedia Commons: Photo by Master Corporal Angela Abbey, Canadian Forces Combat Camera/ISAF Headquarters Public Affairs Office 35, SPC Hilda Clayton 20, Photo by Sgt. Jennifer Cohen/ISAF Headquarters Public Affairs Office 24, Simon Davis/DFID 33, Master Sgt. Tracy DeMarco 40, DoD, DD-ST-88-09407 (Released to Public) 6, Eric Draper/White House 11, Fraz.khalid1 27, Jim Gordon 42, Staff Sgt. Vernell Hall, US Army 28, Staff Sgt. Shane Hamann 25, ISAF Headquarters Public Affairs Office (http://www.flickr.com/people/29456680@N06) from Kabul, Afghanistan 18, Sgt. Frances Johnson 38, Spc. Eric Jungels 21, April Lapetoda 41, SGT Jeremy T. Lock 17, Lt. j. g. Joe Painter/Isafmedia 10, Cpl. Paul Peterson 39, SSgt Cecilio Ricardo, USAF 12, 32, Pete Souza, Official White House Photographer 29, 31, US Air Force photo/Staff Sgt. Aaron Allmon 34, US Army 36, US Army photo by Sgt. Matthew C. Moeller 22, US DoD 26, US Marine Corps photo by Cpl. Chelsea Flowers Anderson 37, US Marine Corps photo by Staff Sgt. William Greeson 23, US Navy photo by Chief Photographer's Mate Johnny Bivera 16, US Navy photo by Captain Dana Potts 13, US Navy photo by Photographer's Mate 1st Class Tim Turner 14, Photo by G. A. Volb/NATO Training Mission Afghanistan 44.

Printed in the United States of America

CONTENTS

CHAPTER 1

WAR ON TERROR

The War in Afghanistan began on October 7, 2001, when the United States and its **ally**, the United Kingdom (UK), invaded Afghanistan. The invasion was a response to the September 11, 2001, attacks on the United States. To fully understand the war, we need to look farther back in time.

Afghanistan is in central Asia. It is bordered by Pakistan to its south and east, and Iran, Turkmenistan, Uzbekistan, Tajikistan, and China to its west and north. It is home to around thirty-three million people, who belong to different ethnic groups and speak their own languages or **dialects**. The largest group is the Pashtuns, who also live over the border in Pakistan. Pashtuns, who speak Pashto, take pride in their warrior history. Other ethnic groups include the Tajiks, Hazara, Uzbeks, Aimaq, Turkmen, and Baloch. More than 99 percent of Afghans are Muslim. A large part of Afghanistan is covered by mountains or desert and is not suitable for farming.

The capital of Afghanistan is Kabul, which has 3.6 million inhabitants.

Droughts, when there is no rain for weeks or months, are frequent in Afghanistan.

Four out of five Afghans rely on farming for a living, and it is a tough life. More than one-third of Afghans live in poverty.

Afghanistan's location, sandwiched between more powerful neighbors, has led to **millennia** of invasion by different conquerors, including Alexander the Great in 330 BCE and Genghis Khan in 1219 CE. In the nineteenth and early twentieth centuries, Afghanistan was caught between two rival **empires**: the British and the Russian. The British ruled India, which included the region of modern Pakistan, while Russia held the land to the north of Afghanistan. Britain invaded Afghanistan three times to try to hold back Russian influence. Finally, in 1919, Britain recognized Afghanistan as a fully independent nation.

In 1947, the British withdrew from India. India was divided into the modern states of Pakistan and India. Afghanistan wanted Pashtuns in Pakistan to be allowed to decide if they wanted to be part of an independent Pashtun state, which Afghanistan hoped one day to take over. Pakistan refused. Looking for powerful support, the Afghan government turned to Russia, which was now the Soviet Union, a **communist** state. The Soviet Union started to have more and more influence in Afghanistan, making reforms such as seizing land and giving it to farmers. These changes were welcomed by Afghan communists but opposed by those who felt that communism was in conflict with Islam. This tussling resulted in Soviet soldiers invading Afghanistan in 1979.

The Soviet Union's **occupation** of Afghanistan was opposed by the Afghan "mujahideen." Mujahideen is the name given to a band of Muslim fighters, particularly those who fight against non-Muslim forces. In Afghanistan, the mujahideen was made up of different tribal groups. Slowly, the groups roughly organized themselves into one opposition to the Soviets. They also gained money and weapons from overseas, including from the United States, which had pledged to fight communism. This was the time of the Cold War, a period of conflict between the United States and its allies, and the Soviet Union and its allies. Some Muslim men from other countries went to Afghanistan to help, including a man from Saudi Arabia named Osama bin Laden. In 1989, the Soviet Union realized it could not win the war against the mujahideen. The war had cost the lives of fourteen thousand Soviet soldiers, eighteen thousand Afghan soldiers loyal to the Soviets, at least seventy-five thousand mujahideen, and more than 850 thousand Afghan **civilians**. Around 3.5 million Afghans had fled to neighboring countries. The Soviet Union withdrew its soldiers, leaving Afghanistan with a weak communist government. The mujahideen fought the government, and each other, for control. This **civil war** resulted in tens of thousands more deaths, the destruction of buildings and facilities, and even greater poverty for civilians. Finally, a group called the Taliban battled its way to power,

An Afghan fighter launches missiles against Soviet forces.

The Northern Alliance banded together from mujahideen who were opposed to the Taliban.

seizing the capital city, Kabul, in September 1996.

However, the Taliban had failed to gain control of northern Afghanistan, which was held by the Northern Alliance, a group assembled from fighters from the Tajik, Hazara, and Uzbek peoples.

A religious teacher and fighter named Mullah Mohammed Omar led the Taliban, which was mostly made up of Pashtuns. "Taliban" means "students" in Pashto. The Taliban believed in the importance of studying the Muslim holy book, the Koran, and following their own strict interpretation of the Koran's teachings. The Taliban were militant Islamists. Militant Islamists believe in using violence when necessary to create an Islamic state, governed according to **Islamic law**.

Not all Afghans believed in the Taliban's strict interpretation of the Koran. Many Afghans felt the Taliban's beliefs were too extreme. Most Muslims believe that violence has no place in Islam, believing instead that their religion is based on love and kindness. However, plenty of Afghans welcomed the Taliban, as they offered an end to war at last.

The Taliban governed Afghanistan according to their interpretation of the Koran. Girls age ten or older were not allowed to go to school. Women had to cover themselves entirely with a **burka**, were forbidden to have jobs, and were not allowed outside the home unless they were accompanied by a male relative. Music and television were banned. Punishments for minor offences included whipping. In 2001, a **United Nations (UN)** report accused the Taliban of deliberately killing large numbers of civilians in its efforts to control northern Iraq.

Osama bin Laden had left Afghanistan after the Soviets withdrew, but in 1996, the Taliban invited him and his men to help take control of the whole country. He was now the leader of a group called al-Qaeda (meaning "The Base"). He declared a jihad (by which he meant a "holy war") to expel non-Muslim soldiers and influences from Islamic lands.

Under Taliban rule, Afghan women had to speak quietly and wear a burka when in public.

Police officers and firefighters work near the Twin Towers on September 11, 2001.

This was a declaration of war against the United States, which had troops stationed in the Middle East. He was angered by the influence of the United States and its allies in the Muslim world, including their support of the Jewish state of Israel. Al-Qaeda set up training camps in eastern Afghanistan, which attracted thousands of militant Islamists from around the world.

In 1998, al-Qaeda bombed the US embassies in the African countries of Tanzania and Kenya, killing 224 people and injuring more than four thousand.

The United States responded by firing missiles at an al-Qaeda training camp in Afghanistan. The UN ordered Afghanistan to hand over Osama bin Laden for trial in the United States, but the Taliban did not obey. Then, on September 11, 2001, **terrorists** from al-Qaeda hijacked two passenger planes and flew them into the Twin Towers of New York's World Trade Center. A third plane was flown into the Pentagon in Virginia. A fourth plane crashed after its passengers battled the hijackers. A total of 2,996 people died in one of the deadliest terrorist attacks the world had ever seen.

On September 20, 2001, the president of the United States, George W. Bush, declared a "War on Terror." This campaign aimed to destroy al-Qaeda and the governments that sheltered them or supplied them with money. He aimed to pursue this campaign using military, political, and legal methods. President Bush demanded that the Taliban, led by Mullah Mohammed Omar, hand over bin Laden and shut down all terrorist training camps in Afghanistan.

Mullah Omar refused to comply with the United States' demands. He said he wanted concrete evidence that bin Laden was linked to the September 11 attacks. The United States saw this as a delaying tactic. President Bush and his team started to put plans in place to invade Afghanistan, remove the Taliban from power, and capture bin Laden. The UK, the United States' long-term ally, immediately promised to help.

These Taliban are armed with rifles. Taliban rules forbid men to shave their beards.

I WITNESS WAR

On September 28, 2001, President George W. Bush was entertaining King Abdullah II, ruler of the Middle Eastern country of Jordan, at the White House. The king promised to stand with the United States against terrorism. President Bush answered a journalist's question about the Taliban, saying:

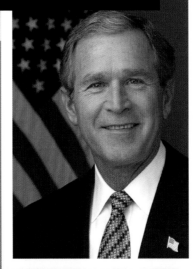

George W. Bush served as president of the United States from 2001 to 2009.

"First, there is no negotiations with the Taliban. They heard what I said. And now they can act. And it's not just Mr. bin Laden that we expect to see and brought to justice; it's everybody associated with his organization that's in Afghanistan. And not only those directly associated with Mr. bin Laden, any terrorist that is housed and fed in Afghanistan needs to be handed over. And finally, we expect there to be complete destruction of terrorist camps. That's what I told them; that's what I mean. And we expect them—we expect them to not only hear what I say but to do something about it."

How would you describe President Bush's language in this extract?

Can you find any words or phrases that express the president's decisiveness?

Does President Bush's manner of speaking remind you of any authority figures in your own life?

CHAPTER 2

TOPPLING THE TALIBAN

The United States and the UK officially started their military operation in Afghanistan on October 7, 2001. The invasion was named "Operation Enduring Freedom." Unknown to the Taliban, operatives from the **Central Intelligence Agency (CIA)** had helicoptered into northern Afghanistan on September 26.

The secret CIA team consisted of seven or eight highly trained men. They spoke the languages of the region and had $3 million in cash to help buy support. The team had been named "Jawbreaker." The men immediately linked up with the leadership of the Northern Alliance. One important Northern Alliance figure was the Uzbek general, Abdul Rashid Dostum. In close contact with both the Northern Alliance and the United States was a Pashtun leader named Hamid Karzai. During the Taliban's rule, he had moved to Pakistan, where he worked to overthrow the Taliban. Now he crossed the border with his men.

The United States felt it was vital to join forces with the Northern Alliance and other tribal groups.

Northern Alliance fighters under the command of General Doshtum gather in northern Afghanistan.

These anti-Taliban forces numbered at least fifteen thousand fighters, and there were probably many more who would join the fighting later. This meant that fewer US and UK soldiers would have to take part. However, some human rights organizations questioned the decision to work with the Northern Alliance, as some of their **warlords** had been accused of human rights abuses against those who opposed them. Over the following days and weeks, the Northern Alliance was given weapons and equipment. Together with US and UK forces, a plan was laid out for taking Taliban strongholds. It was estimated that there were around forty-five thousand Taliban soldiers.

On October 7, the United States and the UK began the war when their warplanes fired missiles and dropped bombs on Taliban and al-Qaeda targets. Missiles were also fired from US Navy warships and submarines. The bombings focused on training camps, command bases, and communications. The Taliban's weak air defenses (equipment that would have allowed them to shoot down enemy planes) were destroyed. For Afghan civilians, US planes also dropped food, medicine, and **propaganda**, aimed at persuading Afghans to reject the Taliban.

Around 2,500 US and a few hundred UK forces flew in to support the Northern Alliance. They were Special Forces rather than regular, conventional soldiers. Special Forces include soldiers who are highly skilled at secret and dangerous operations. The US and UK forces were part of a **coalition** force under the overall leadership of US General Tommy Franks. Sometimes the coalition fought alongside the Northern Alliance. At other times, it carried out separate operations against particular targets.

By late October, the Northern Alliance, helped by US and UK warplanes and soldiers, had started to push back Taliban forces from northern Afghanistan. The Taliban were bombarded by some of the most up-to-date technology the coalition owned, including Special Operations Forces Laser Markers (SOFLAMs). These are devices that take aim using lasers, following up with a "smart bomb," guided by **satellite**. "Daisy Cutter" bombs were also used, which explode just above ground, unlike conventional bombs, which explode upon hitting the ground. Daisy Cutters cause maximum casualties. The Taliban had no such advanced weaponry, although they did have tanks, rifles, grenades, and rocket launchers.

The Northern Alliance advanced south toward Kabul. On November 12, as the Northern Alliance approached, most Taliban soldiers fled the city. The following day, after a brief battle with a small group of fighters, the Northern Alliance took control. Many residents of Kabul greeted the Northern Alliance with gifts, flowers, and cheering. Some celebrated by playing music, which was no longer forbidden. However, others were afraid that the future would hold as much fear as the past.

A member of US Special Forces surveys the Afghan landscape.

I WITNESS WAR

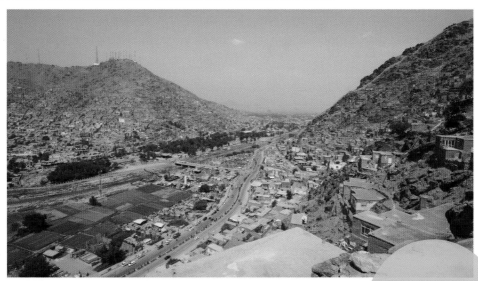

Scott Peterson, a US reporter for *The Christian Science Monitor*, was with the Northern Alliance when they entered Kabul. On November, 14, 2001, he wrote about what he witnessed, describing the joy of the Northern Alliance and many Kabul civilians. He ended his article with the words:

"… a family buried Taliban Commander Mahmoud, who was killed in the fighting. The grave was dug into a hillside, and Mahmoud's wife and brother sobbed as the body was lowered into the hole and covered with broad shale stones, then dirt."

What does the word "family" suggest to you?

Do any of the words in the extract make you feel sympathy for Commander Mahmoud's family?

Why do you think Scott Peterson ended his article by mentioning the Taliban?

By the end of November, the surviving Taliban soldiers had retreated to southern Afghanistan, around the large city of Kandahar. This was the home of Mullah Omar, their leader. Northern Alliance and other Afghan tribal forces, led in part by Hamid Karzai, **besieged** the city. On December 7, Kandahar was captured, but Mullah Omar had escaped. The fall of Kandahar marked the end of the Taliban's rule. To help keep order, the United States built military bases close to major Afghan cities.

The majority of the remaining Taliban soldiers were not captured. They fled into Afghanistan's mountainous countryside or across the border to Pakistan, where some of them had family or other links. The far western region of Pakistan, bordering Afghanistan, is mountainous and remote. Mullah Omar and some of the Taliban's surviving leadership settled near the Pakistani city of Quetta.

The United States believed that bin Laden and some al-Qaeda fighters were hiding in a cave complex called Tora Bora, in the mountainous far east of Afghanistan. From December 6–17, coalition Special Forces and Afghan fighters battled to get into the complex. When they finally did, there was no sign of bin Laden.

An Afghan tribal fighter wraps a bandolier of ammunition around his body during a joint operation with US Marines.

Canadian soldiers join the hunt for Osama bin Laden in the Tora Bora region.

The United States suspected that bin Laden had been in the caves but escaped to Pakistan, perhaps with the help of an Afghan tribal leader who was supposedly fighting on the side of the United States. Al-Qaeda set up new bases in Pakistan's northwestern mountains.

The number of deaths among coalition soldiers during fall 2001 is carefully recorded: Twelve US soldiers died. The number of deaths among Afghan civilians is estimated, but the number was almost certainly more than two thousand. More than one thousand civilian deaths were recorded as a result of US and UK bombings. Other civilians died while trying to flee the battlegrounds, from exposure, illness, or injury. Not all such deaths are recorded, so some estimates put the number of civilian deaths far higher than two thousand. The number of deaths among Taliban and Northern Alliance forces is also estimated. Northern Alliance casualties were probably in the hundreds, while Taliban casualties numbered in the thousands.

In December 2001, while fighting continued in Afghanistan, Afghan leaders who had opposed the Taliban, along with international leaders, met at a conference organized by the UN in Bonn, Germany. They agreed on terms for an interim (temporary) government to run Afghanistan until nationwide elections could be held.

The United States nominated Hamid Karzai to lead the interim government. He had a good relationship with the United States. He was also a moderate Pashtun, which was Afghanistan's largest ethnic group, and he was not linked with the violence carried out by some Northern Alliance warlords. The conference voted that he would head the government and lead the drawing up of a constitution for Afghanistan. Karzai was fighting outside Kandahar at the time, but he accepted his election by satellite phone. When Karzai took on responsibility for his country, it was in a terrible state. The previous two decades of war, since the Soviet invasion, had killed at least one million Afghans. Few hospitals were still standing, and most doctors and nurses had left the county. The lack of medical care meant that, according to a 2002 United Nations International Children's Fund (UNICEF) report, around 500 thousand women died in childbirth every year. The World Bank reported that, in 2001, only 21 percent of children, all of them boys, went to elementary school. The UN said that only 4.8 percent of the population had access to safe drinking water.

When Hamid Karzai became interim president, the life expectancy for Afghans was fifty-five years old.

In 2001, around thirteen out of every hundred children born in Afghanistan died by the age of five.

Finally, after debate in the loya jirga, a traditional council of Afghan tribal leaders, the new constitution was agreed upon in January 2004. It set the terms for a state run in line with moderate Islamic principles. A register of all Afghans older than the age of eighteen was drawn up. Elections for president were held in October. In all its previous history, Afghanistan had only had a **democracy** for nine years, between 1964 and 1973. Voters now had the choice of seventeen men, including Karzai, and one woman. Karzai won and put together a government for the newly named Islamic Republic of Afghanistan.

19

CHAPTER 3

THE TALIBAN FIGHTS BACK

With Afghanistan in ruins, the new Afghan government and its international supporters faced an uphill struggle to maintain peace and reconstruct the country. For now, much power lay in the hands of the Afghan warlords who had helped drive out the Taliban. However, the Taliban and al-Qaeda had not given up. They were gathering strength in hiding.

On December 20, 2001, the UN had agreed on an international force of around five thousand soldiers to help the Afghans keep order in and around Kabul, and to help rebuild public buildings and facilities. It was called the International Security Assistance Force (ISAF). A coalition of eighteen countries sent soldiers to join the force, including the United States, the UK, Australia, Canada, Germany, and France. Other US and UK soldiers remained under the direct control of their own commanders. By this point, the United States had sent a total of seven thousand soldiers to Afghanistan, many of them now conventional soldiers rather than Special Forces.

The ISAF's job was also to help train a new Afghan National Army and police force, so that the government would not have to rely on warlords to keep control. The first 1,750 Afghan National Army soldiers went on duty in 2003. Over the following ten years, their number grew to 200 thousand.

During most of 2002, the Taliban lay low in southeastern Afghanistan, as well as over the border in western Pakistan. These were areas largely inhabited by Pashtuns. The new

Afghan National Army soldiers take part in a training exercise.

A US soldier patrols through Nuristan province in eastern Afghanistan.

Afghan government's control did not fully stretch to these mountainous regions where tribal leaders had always held sway. The same was true for the Pakistani government in parts of western Pakistan, where the Taliban and groups allied to them were gaining power. Although many Taliban soldiers had died during the fall of 2001, many more were now being recruited. The ISAF, US, and Afghan forces led patrols and raids into the mountains, but usually, the Taliban was able to escape them. During September 2002, Taliban pamphlets were secretly distributed in southeastern Afghanistan. These pamphlets urged Pashtuns to rise up in jihad against the new order.

Some Afghans were growing unhappy because a number of civilians had been killed by ISAF and US **air strikes**, which were intended to kill Taliban and al-Qaeda fighters. Some farmers were also upset as the coalition soldiers tried to stop them from growing poppies, an important source of their income. Poppies can be used to manufacture opium and heroin, which are illegal narcotics. An Afghan farmer earns, on average, around $200 a year. However, growing and selling poppies can increase those earnings to $15,000 a year. This unhappiness encouraged some Afghans to join the antigovernment forces.

In 2003, the Taliban were strong enough to set up training camps and command bases along the border between Afghanistan and Pakistan. Mullah Omar put in place a leadership council and allotted his commanders different areas of southeastern Afghanistan. These commanders started to organize attacks against Afghan and coalition forces. The Taliban used the tactics of guerrilla war. Guerrilla fighters work in small groups, ambushing the enemy, then taking cover again. Al-Qaeda forces in eastern Afghanistan also started to launch ambushes against US troops.

Afghanistan's landscape made guerrilla warfare highly effective. It became clear to the coalition and Afghan government that they were facing an insurgency (rebellion) against the new order.

Command of the UN's ISAF had passed from country to country every six months, as was traditional. However, there were problems in finding new countries to take the lead each time. To solve the issue, in August 2003, the **North Atlantic Treaty Organization (NATO)** took control of the ISAF from the UN. To battle the growing insurgency,

US forces fire mortar rounds at a suspected Taliban position.

A US Marine treats an Afghan boy for a head injury.

the ISAF was expanded to include soldiers from a coalition of fifty-one countries, and the number of soldiers steadily climbed. The soldiers were under the overall command of the United States. By the end of 2004, the United States had increased its soldiers in Afghanistan to sixteen thousand. The ISAF took command of the western portion of Afghanistan in 2005.

The Taliban's targets were not just the soldiers who fought against them but also newly trained Afghan police officers and anyone else who supported the government of Hamid Karzai. Weapons used by the Taliban and al-Qaeda included rifles and rocket launchers. They also made improvised explosive devices (IEDs). These homemade bombs are hidden on roads or in buildings, and they are usually set off on contact, when a vehicle or person travels over them. A timer can also be used to set them off. Someone caught in an IED blast may be killed or may suffer life-changing injuries, such as the loss of limbs. Between 2001 and 2016, IEDs killed around 1,400 coalition soldiers. They also caused many deaths and injuries to Afghan civilians, often among children playing. One estimate is that one-quarter of the thirty-two thousand civilians killed during the conflict were killed by IEDs.

From 2004 onward, the Taliban and al-Qaeda carried out suicide bombings, which were a terrifyingly effective way of killing people in Afghanistan's towns and cities. A suicide bomber detonates explosives that they wear while walking or driving toward the victims. In 2004, there were 6 suicide bombings. In 2005, there were 21, and in 2006, 141. The victims of these attacks were coalition or Afghan soldiers, police officers, politicians, and a large number of ordinary Afghan men, women, and children. By 2006, the death toll among Afghan civilians was steadily increasing. As many as one thousand civilians died that year. Human Rights Watch estimated that at least seven hundred of those deaths were the result of Taliban attacks. At least 230 civilians died during US and ISAF attacks and air strikes.

The ISAF stepped up its attempts to kill or capture Taliban members. In Operation Mountain Thrust, from May to July 2006, ISAF and Afghan National Army troops launched a major offensive against the Taliban in southern Afghanistan. More than one thousand Taliban soldiers were killed, and several hundred were captured. However, the insurgency was showing no signs of stopping. In fact, it was now raging out of control. In the face of the growing violence, the ISAF took command of the south and then the east of Afghanistan during 2006. During that year, 191 coalition soldiers died.

Children ask US soldiers for candy as they pass through a village in the Kunar Valley.

Civilians injured in a suicide bomb are flown off for treatment.

I WITNESS WAR

On March 12, 2006, in Kabul, two suicide bombers attempted to kill Sibghatullah Mojaddedi, a member of the Afghan parliament. Mojaddedi survived, but four passersby were killed. Walking home with her brother and sister, a nine-year-old girl was seriously injured by **shrapnel**. We will call her "Sharzad" as her family want to keep her identity secret. She later spoke about her experience:

"I remember the explosion throwing me a few meters ... I did not feel getting hit by the bomb. The bomb threw me down, but then I stood up and ran away, but then I fell down again ... Sometimes I dream about that day—I have nightmares. I thought that I would not survive. I started saying the Kalimah [prayer said by the dying] when I was hurt that day, because I thought I was going to die, but my brother told me to stop."

Why do you think Sharzad's brother stopped her from saying the prayer for the dying?

What emotions do you think Sharzad's parents felt when they heard she was injured?

Why do you think Sharzad's family is afraid to let her real name be known?

25

CHAPTER 4

FINDING BIN LADEN

For years after the invasion of Afghanistan, the United States thought that Osama bin Laden might be hiding in Pakistan but could not be sure. Perhaps we will never know the full story of how bin Laden was tracked down, as the lives of **informers** and agents may be at risk. The following story is the official version.

As the coalition captured al-Qaeda fighters, the CIA took away their leaders for **interrogation**. The rules for the interrogation of prisoners of war are laid down by international law. However, it later emerged that some of the methods used by the CIA to interrogate prisoners, such as depriving them of sleep for long periods, were cruel. Human rights organizations said that they broke international law and that this amounted to torture.

During their interrogations, the CIA was particularly keen to hear about bin Laden's couriers. Since bin Laden did not use the phone or internet, as these would allow

This is a plan of Osama bin Laden's house in Abbottabad, Pakistan.

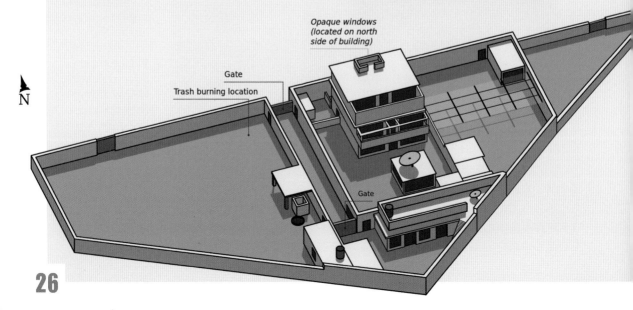

Opaque windows (located on north side of building)

Gate

Trash burning location

Gate

N

Abbottabad is a beautiful, hilly city in northern Pakistan.

him to be traced, trusted couriers carried messages to and from him. A few prisoners mentioned a courier known by the **pseudonym** al-Kuwaiti ("the man from Kuwait"). The CIA then asked two top-level al-Qaeda prisoners, who had been close to bin Laden, if they knew of al-Kuwaiti. Both said they had never heard of him. The CIA did not think it likely that they really did not know the man. This made them believe al-Kuwaiti was very important indeed. The CIA eventually managed to find out al-Kuwaiti's family name. This allowed them to trace the courier's family. The CIA started to monitor emails and phone calls between the family and anyone in Pakistan. Using the information they learned, they discovered the courier's full name: Ibrahim Saeed Ahmed. In July 2010, Pakistani agents working for the CIA spotted al-Kuwaiti's car near Peshawar, in Pakistan. The agents followed him for several weeks. Eventually, he drove to a large house in the city of Abbottabad, Pakistan. Tall concrete walls topped with barbed wire surrounded the house. Everyone had imagined that Osama bin Laden would be hiding in a remote mountain cave. Could bin Laden really be living in a wealthy suburb in Abbottabad?

For weeks, the house was watched from the ground and from spy satellites. Various people were seen coming and going, but not bin Laden. The inhabitants burned all their garbage. They had no phone line or internet access. These facts were suspicious. President Barack Obama, who had taken over the presidency after George W. Bush in 2009, was made aware of the situation. The CIA, military, and White House discussed options for how to bring bin Laden to justice, if he was in the house. They knew they would have to launch a sudden attack, so bin Laden would not be able to escape, as he had at Tora Bora. One option was an air strike, but that would destroy the entire house, leaving no evidence of whether or not bin Laden had been there. Instead, they decided on a helicopter assault.

A team of Navy SEALS ("Sea, Air, and Land" special operations force) went into training. On Sunday May 1, 2011, guided tours around the White House were canceled. President Obama, Secretary of State Hillary Clinton, and other important officials gathered in the White House Situation Room to watch the CIA chief, Leon Panetta, narrate the progress of the operation from CIA headquarters in Langley, Virginia. It had been decided not to warn the

Black Hawk helicopters carried the SEALS to the raid on bin Laden's hideout.

President Obama (*second from left*), Vice President Joe Biden (*far left*), and the national security team gathered tensely in the Situation Room.

Pakistani government of the raid in case the news leaked out to bin Laden. For that reason, the US Navy helicopters, which were taking off from Afghanistan, had to cross the border and back again very quickly. If not, the Pakistani government might think the helicopters were being piloted by terrorists and might attack them.

Soon after midnight in Pakistan, around twenty-four SEALs jumped out of two helicopters and stormed into the house in Abbottabad. Some reports say the inhabitants of the house fired weapons at the SEALs, while other reports say they were mostly unarmed. Four people were killed in the first few minutes: bin Laden's son, Khalid; al-Kuwaiti; and al-Kuwaiti's brother and sister-in-law. Also in the house were four of bin Laden's wives, nine of his children and grandchildren, and four children in al-Kuwaiti's family. Two of bin Laden's wives were wounded, but the children were not hurt. On the third floor, the SEALs found a man who looked like bin Laden. Again, reports differ as to whether or not he was armed and tried to defend himself. One or more bullets to the head killed him. The code name for bin Laden was "Geronimo." The SEAL team leader radioed, "Geronimo EKIA." "EKIA" stands for "enemy killed in action."

It was now vital to make sure the man killed was definitely bin Laden. The SEALs took a photo of the dead man's face and sent it to Langley. The photo was processed through **facial recognition software**, confirming with near certainty that it was bin Laden. Later, DNA tests compared the man's DNA with known relatives of bin Laden and confirmed a match with 99.9 percent certainty. Taking the body with them, the Seals took off in one of their helicopters, just as Pakistani forces were rushing to the site. The raid had taken 38 minutes.

President Obama wanted to follow Islamic tradition, so bin Laden needed to be buried within 24 hours of dying. Since the president did not want to create a shrine for bin Laden's followers to flock to, it was decided to bury him at sea. The body was washed and wrapped according to Islamic tradition and, as prayers were said in Arabic, slid into the sea from the warship USS *Carl Vinson*. Human rights groups questioned whether it had been necessary to kill bin Laden, as everyone, no matter what their crimes, has a right to a fair trial. US officials said they would have taken bin Laden alive if he had not resisted being captured.

The killing of Osama bin Laden made headlines all around the world.

I WITNESS WAR

On the night of May 2, 2011, President Barack Obama addressed the nation. He announced the death of Osama bin Laden and spoke about the ongoing battle against terrorism. This is an extract from his speech:

President Obama announces the death of Osama bin Laden.

"... The American people did not choose this fight. It came to our shores and started with the senseless slaughter of our citizens. After nearly ten years of service, struggle, and sacrifice, we know well the costs of war. These efforts weigh on me every time I, as Commander-in-Chief, have to sign a letter to a family that has lost a loved one, or look into the eyes of a service member who's been gravely wounded. So Americans understand the costs of war. Yet, as a country, we will never tolerate our security being threatened, nor stand idly by when our people have been killed. ... And on nights like this one, we can say to those families who have lost loved ones to al-Qaeda's terror: Justice has been done. ..."

What words would you use to describe the tone of President Obama's speech?

Why do you think he uses the phrase "look into the eyes"?

In this extract, President Obama repeats one particular phrase. Why do you think that is?

CHAPTER 5

BATTLING FOR CONTROL

The international coalition hoped to hand over security for Afghanistan to the Afghan National Army. However, the Taliban's power was growing rather than shrinking. From 2006 to 2012, the ISAF had to increase the number of coalition soldiers in Afghanistan again and again. The ISAF also increased its efforts to rebuild facilities for Afghans.

The Taliban continued to fight the Afghan government and coalition using IEDs, suicide bombs, ambushes, and the killing of government officials. They also employed the tactic of "turncoat" killings: Members joined the Afghan National Army or police force, then turned their weapons on their fellows. The ISAF and Afghan National Army continued to fight back with air strikes, raids, patrols, and searches. However, the Taliban's efforts were paying off. The ISAF could not patrol every village, street, and city market.

Larger parts of Afghanistan came under Taliban control. The Afghan government's efforts to rebuild were often thwarted. Suicide bombings made people afraid to oppose the Taliban, or to be caught close to someone who did. For example,

A US soldier talks to children in a camp in Kabul for Afghans who had fled the fighting.

on February 17, 2008, a suicide bomb in Kandahar was aimed at killing the local police chief. Around one hundred civilians also died in the attack. One of the Taliban's most high-profile successes was on June 13, 2008, when Taliban forces managed to free all 1,200 of the prisoners in Sarposa Prison, Kandahar. Around four hundred of them were Taliban. This demonstration of the Taliban's strength left the ISAF embarrassed and worried.

By the fall of 2009, General Stanley McChrystal, newly appointed as US commander in Afghanistan, said he thought the Taliban had gained the upper hand. The Taliban were now even putting in place their own regional governments in the parts of Afghanistan they controlled. To make matters worse, there were also several other groups that had allied themselves with the Taliban, including al-Qaeda and the Haqqani network, led by the fighter Jalaluddin Haqqani. Over the border in Pakistan, the Pakistani Taliban were battling with the Pakistani Army for control of the Swat Valley. One of the Taliban's most famous actions in valley was the shooting in the head of fifteen-year-old education campaigner Malala Yousafzai. She later made an almost complete recovery in the UK.

Malala Yousafzai was shot because she campaigned for girls' education.

Only a small proportion of Afghans were in favor of the Taliban. The majority just wanted to live safely with their families and have a job and food to eat. However, although most Afghans had supported the US-led invasion at first, many now wished the foreigners would leave. One main reason was the high number of civilian casualties of the conflict, some at the hands of the coalition itself. For example, on September 4, 2009, a US fighter jet mistakenly fired on two fuel tankers that had been captured by the Taliban, near Kunduz in northern Afghanistan. The resulting explosion killed around one hundred people, including at least seventy civilians, many of them children. In 2010,

the number of civilians killed hit its peak since 2001, with at least 2,777 deaths. Of those deaths, the UN Mission in Afghanistan estimated that more than two thousand were caused by the Taliban and other insurgents. At least 440 were caused by the ISAF. Afghans were also deeply concerned by **corruption** in the Afghan government. Everyone was frustrated by the slow pace of the rebuilding of hospitals, schools, transportation, and services such as water treatment. People were asking if the government was working as hard as it could. Many suspected that some government officials were becoming rich from the international donations that should have been spent on reconstruction.

It was an F-15E Strike Eagle fighter that accidentally killed many civilians near Kunduz.

A US soldier reaches out to Afghan women during the Muslim festival of Eid.

In 2009, presidential elections were held for a second time since the Islamic Republic of Afghanistan had been created. Hamid Karzai won again, but there were widespread claims of fraud (cheating) and intimidation during the process. On election day, as a result of violence and the threat of violence from the Taliban, only around one-third of adult Afghans voted. All of these problems weakened the Afghan government and made some people more willing to turn to those who fought against them.

By the end of 2010, the number of ISAF troops had been increased to 120 thousand. The number of US soldiers reached a peak at ninety thousand and UK soldiers at 9,500. Germany, France, Italy, Canada, and Poland were also major contributors of soldiers, with more than two thousand each. There were now four hundred ISAF bases in Afghanistan and three hundred Afghan National Army or Afghan National Police bases, most of them built or supported by the coalition. General McChrystal said he believed the tide was turning, with some towns and regions being brought back under ISAF control. However, as the ISAF took control of Helmand province in the south, the Taliban moved soldiers to the north, seizing new areas in provinces such as Kunduz.

35

At home in the United States and other coalition countries, people were worried about the number of soldiers being sent to Afghanistan. They were also deeply worried about the soldiers who were dying or injured. By the end of 2010, 1,365 US, 348 UK, and 154 Canadian soldiers had died, with another 414 deaths among other countries of the coalition. When the invasion began, several thousand people in the United States had demonstrated against the war. However, there had been fairly broad support for the war in the United States, UK, and UN. As the war dragged on, at huge human and financial cost, support for the war was fading. In the United States, more people began to liken the war to the Vietnam War (1955–1975), a lengthy and unpopular overseas war that caused high numbers of casualties. The size of protests against the war increased, the protests often combined with those against the War in Iraq (2003–2011).

The Afghan government and the coalition agreed that the best option would be to set a timetable for handing over security in Afghanistan to the Afghan National Army and police. On November 20, 2010, NATO announced that the ISAF would withdraw its troops by 2014. The United States promised to start withdrawing soldiers from 2011. Yet the question remained: Would the Afghan National Army be able to defeat the Taliban without help?

US soldiers honor their fallen comrades.

I WITNESS WAR

Having lost limbs from IEDs, these veterans are using running blades to train together.

On December 12, 2012, US Army Captain Jason Pak was leading his men on a patrol when he stepped on an IED. He lost both his legs and two fingers in the blast. He later spoke about what he remembers of the moment the bomb went off:

"The last thing I remember, I think I stepped on that mound and it, it went off. Immediately when it happened, I got knocked back. Um, my right hand was with my rifle, my left hand was out, I'm also a left partial amputee, I lost a couple of fingers. My eardrums were blown out, I can't hear anything. I just hear a flatline beep. And then, as a couple seconds go by, I can start hearing people yelling … 'Sir, you're going to be all right.'"

Does this account have any similarities with Sharzad's account on page 25?

What emotions do you think Captain Pak felt in the aftermath of the attack?

How do you think Captain Pak felt when he heard a friendly voice?

CHAPTER 6

AFGHANISTAN TODAY

The United States and other coalition countries had withdrawn most of their soldiers from Afghanistan by December 28, 2014. This officially marked the end of the US-led War in Afghanistan. However, the Taliban did not halt their war against the Afghan government. Today, life in Afghanistan is still dangerous and very difficult.

As agreed between the Afghan government and the coalition, ISAF forces stopped **combat missions** in Afghanistan by the middle of 2013. Combat missions were taken over by the Afghan National Army. The ISAF remained until December 2014 to train and advise Afghan soldiers and police officers. However, since everyone agreed that Afghanistan would continue to need help keeping order, a new NATO mission, called Operation Resolute Support, took over a support role from December 28, 2014.

Around thirteen thousand international soldiers took part in Operation Resolute Support, with the largest number from the United States. The majority of the force was employed in training Afghan security forces, but some also undertook combat missions against insurgents. US air strikes against the Taliban and other insurgents continued. In 2015 and 2016, air strikes killed an estimated 2,400–3,000 people, of whom around

The Afghan National Army took over most operations from coalition forces.

Several thousand US soldiers remained in Afghanistan to back up Afghan security forces.

125 were civilians. Initially, Operation Resolute Support was intended to last until 2016, but it was extended indefinitely because of the continuing insurgency.

On September 28, 2015, the Taliban seemed to have a breakthrough when it seized Kunduz. This was the first time it had controlled a major city since 2001. Afghan and NATO forces took back the city on October 14. According to UN estimates, at least 848 civilians were killed during the battle for Kunduz. During 2015 and 2016, the Taliban also captured large parts of Helmand province, but it was held back from further gains by Afghan and NATO forces.

The ongoing war continued to cause a high number of deaths and injuries. In 2015 and 2016, it is estimated that up to thirty-five thousand insurgent fighters may have been killed. During the same period, twelve thousand Afghan soldiers, thirty-three US soldiers, and seven other NATO soldiers were killed. At least 6,500 civilians died and 800 thousand were forced to flee their homes. Taliban suicide bombs continued to make Afghans fearful as they went about their lives. For example, on April 19, 2016, an attack against Afghan security forces killed sixty-four people and wounded 347 in Kabul.

When the United States invaded Afghanistan, it had three aims, which were closely linked. The US government wanted to find Osama bin Laden, destroy al-Qaeda, and topple the Taliban. When considering the War in Afghanistan, we can question whether the United States succeeded in meeting those aims and whether meeting them was worth the human cost. First of all, we can begin to glimpse the human cost of the war by looking at statistics.

Between 2001 and 2016, the War in Afghanistan caused the deaths of somewhere between forty thousand and seventy-five thousand Taliban, al-Qaeda, and other antigovernment forces. At least thirty-four thousand Afghan National Army soldiers, police officers, and Northern Alliance fighters died. Among the forces of the international coalition, 3,526 died and more than twenty-two thousand were wounded. The deaths of 32,815 civilians were officially recorded between 2001 and 2016; many other deaths from injury, illness, and hunger may have gone unrecorded. By the end of 2015, the United Nations Refugee Agency estimated there were 1.2 million "internally displaced" people in Afghanistan. These were people forced to flee their homes and live elsewhere in Afghanistan, in the homes of family and friends, in makeshift shelters, or in camps provided by the government or international charities. Many displaced Afghans have little access to drinking water, schools, medical care, and jobs. There were also 2.7 million Afghan **refugees** overseas, in Iran, Pakistan, and in countries such as Germany, the UK, and the United States. Some have since returned home.

Children line up for blankets and warm clothes in a camp for displaced people in western Afghanistan.

I WITNESS WAR

An Albanian soldier carries a child's bag of supplies in a camp in Kabul.

In November 2015, the human rights organization Amnesty International interviewed a sixteen-year-old girl named Freshta. She was living in Chaman-e-Babrak, a camp for internally displaced people in Kabul. She said:

"I've been here since I was a child. Since I was a little kid, I've always had to struggle. I could never go to school, there was no time, as I had to make a living. Survival always came first."

Find out more about the situation for children in Afghanistan today. How is it different from your life?

How would you feel if you "could never go to school"?

Why do you think Freshta "had to make a living"?

A main aim of the war was to topple the Taliban. The Taliban were successfully removed from power in Kabul within a few weeks of the 2001 invasion. However, in 2017, the Taliban, al-Qaeda, and other insurgent groups still held large pockets of territory in Afghanistan, amounting to around one-third of the country. The ongoing conflict with the Taliban continued to take lives and prevent progress in Afghanistan. The Afghan government had offered to have peace talks with the Taliban since 2010. The Taliban refused to take part until the coalition had withdrawn its soldiers. In July 2015, the first talks between the Afghan government and Taliban took place. No progress was made, but there were some hopes that the Taliban would one day accept a peace agreement. Some people had begun to say that, even among the Taliban leadership, there was a growing realization that the war could not be won outright by either side. The Taliban had lost huge numbers of

Al-Qaeda members in Iraq killed hundreds of civilians with car bombs between 2004 and 2006.

In Nice, France, flowers are left for the eighty-six people killed by an Islamic State attack on July 14, 2016.

the Taliban in Afghanistan. Al-Qaeda terrorists still carry out attacks around the world. One example is the March 2004 al-Qaeda bombing of commuter trains in Madrid, Spain, which killed 190 people. The terrorist group Islamic State grew from al-Qaeda's branch in Iraq. From 2013, Islamic State seized large territories in Syria and Iraq. It became well known for its attacks on civilians in heavily Islamic populations and elsewhere. One of its many attacks took place in November 2015, when 130 people were killed in Paris, France.

men and several of its leaders to the fight. However, it had continued to recruit more. Taliban leader Mullah Omar died from tuberculosis in 2013. He was succeeded by Akhtar Mansour, who was killed in a US **drone** strike in 2016. Mansour was succeeded by Hibatullah Akhundzada. Perhaps another reason to hope the Taliban would negotiate was that fewer people were willing to donate money to them after 2014. This was because the Taliban's victims were no longer usually foreign soldiers but were often Afghan civilians.

In its aims of capturing bin Laden and destroying al-Qaeda, was the United States successful? Although bin Laden was killed in 2011, al-Qaeda fighters still battle alongside

Since President George W. Bush declared the start of the War on Terror, terrorist attacks around the world have increased. The Global Terrorism Index reports that there were 3,361 terrorist attacks in 2000. In 2013, there were 17,958. Some Afghans argue that the US-led invasion encouraged some people to turn to militant Islamist groups. They argue that militant Islamism is a way of thinking rather than a particular group of people. By that reasoning, it is unlikely to be wiped out by military action.

A final question to ask is whether life in Afghanistan is better today than it was in 2001, before the US-led invasion. Today, Afghans have the right to elect their leaders and have a say in how their country is run. However, many Afghans are concerned about government corruption, while others wonder if their new democracy is more suited to a Western nation than an Islamic one. In September 2014, Ashraf Ghani was elected as the new president of Afghanistan. He pledged to fight corruption and give greater rights to women and girls. In 2001, almost no girls went to school. In 2017, there were 2.5 million girls in school. However, there were still three million children overall with no access to a school. Women are slowly making their way into the workforce: In 2017, women filled around one in six jobs. Today, there are female police officers, doctors, lawyers, and politicians.

In 2001, Afghanistan was suffering from widespread poverty following decades of war. There was poor access to medical care, and the situation was soon worsened by the invasion. Today, many hospitals have been rebuilt, medicines distributed, vaccinations given, and **sanitation** improved. However, with

In 2017, around one-third of all schoolchildren were girls.

an average life expectancy of sixty years old, Afghanistan has a long way to go. In the United States, life expectancy is seventy-nine.

Afghanistan remains one of the world's poorest countries. Afghanistan's government, Afghan businesspeople, and the international community are working to improve farming methods and to create new jobs in industries such as construction, manufacturing, and mining. However, 40 percent of people were unemployed in 2015, not including the many women not actively seeking jobs. Poverty and patchy government control had led at least 200 thousand Afghan farmers to grow poppies, which are sold at a high price and made into heroin. Afghan heroin was supplying around eleven million drug addicts worldwide. Afghanistan risked becoming a country that relies on drugs for its income.

Between 2001 and 2017, the international community, including many Afghans living abroad, gave $100 billion to rebuild Afghanistan. To keep improving the lives of Afghans, many more billions will need to be spent, and Afghanistan's government and people will have to continue to battle.

WAR STORY

To find out more about the War in Afghanistan and to consider some of the issues raised by the conflict, write your own "eyewitness" account of an event during the war.

1. Which event will you write about? Perhaps you could choose the day the Northern Alliance entered Kabul or the moment the last US soldiers withdrew in 2014.

2. Research your chosen event, using books in your school and local library. With the help of an adult, you could search the web: be aware that many websites about the War in Afghanistan contain graphic images and information.

3. From what point of view will you write your account? You could choose a soldier, civilian, charity worker, or politician.

4. What form will your account take? It could be a journalist's report (as on page 15), a public speech (as on pages 11 or 31), or a "spoken" firsthand account (as on pages 25, 37, and 41).

GLOSSARY

air strikes Attacks made by aircraft.

ally Country or group that helps another country or group.

besieged Surrounded a place with armed force.

burka A loose garment that covers the wearer from head to toe, revealing only the eyes.

Central Intelligence Agency (CIA) A US government security agency that works outside the United States.

civilians People who are not in the armed forces or police force.

civil war A war between organized groups in the same country.

coalition A group of people or countries that have joined together for a shared purpose.

combat missions Missions during which another armed force is fought.

communist A country or person that follows the principles of communism, in which all property is shared by the community.

corruption Misuse of power.

democracy A political system in which a country's people vote for their leader.

dialects Forms of a language belonging to a particular region.

drone A remotely piloted aircraft.

empires Groups of countries under the rule of one government.

facial recognition software A computer program that identifies people using images of them.

informers People who provide information about others.

interrogation Questioning someone.

Islamic law A code of law based on the Muslim holy book, the Koran.

life expectancy The average number of years that a person is expected to live.

millenia Thousands of years.

NATO (North Atlantic Treaty Organization) A military alliance of twenty-eight member states in North America and Europe.

occupation Control of a foreign territory by armed forces.

propaganda Information used to promote a particular point of view.

pseudonym A name used by someone in place of their real name.

refugees People forced to leave their country to escape war, persecution, or natural disaster.

sanitation The supply of clean water and treatment of human waste.

satellite An electronic device that moves around Earth.

shrapnel Fragments thrown out by an explosion.

terrorists People who use violence to achieve their political aims.

United Nations (UN) An international organization with 193 independent states as members.

warlords Military leaders who hold complete power over their territory.

FURTHER READING

BOOKS

Doeden, Matt, and Blake Hoena. *War in Afghanistan: An Interactive Modern History Adventure* (You Choose: Modern History). North Mankato, MN: Capstone Press, 2014.

Nardo, Don. *Understanding Afghanistan Today* (A Kid's Guide to the Middle East). Hallandale, FL: Mitchell Lane Publishing Inc., 2014.

Steele, Philip. *Afghanistan: From War to Peace? (Our World Divided)*. New York: Rosen Central, 2012.

WEBSITES

Time for Kids
http://timeforkids.com/destination/afghanistan
Find out about Afghanistan and the people who live there.

UNICEF
http://unicef.org/afghanistan
Read about UNICEF's assessment of the situation for children in Afghanistan.

United Nations Refugee Agency
http://unhcr.org
Discover more about refugees and the work of the UN Refugee Agency.

The White House
http://obamawhitehouse.archives.gov/blog/2011/05/02/osama-bin-laden-dead
Read President Barack Obama's full address to the nation when he announced the death of Osama bin Laden on May 2, 2011.

INDEX

Acknowledgments:
The publisher would like to thank the following people for permission to use their material:
p. 11 President George W. Bush, speaking at a photo opportunity, The Oval Office, Washington, DC, September 28, 2001, https://2001-2009.state.gov/coalition/cr/rm/2001/5114.htm, p. 15 Scott Peterson, "Taliban Yield Kabul, But Not War," November 14, 2001, the Christian Science Monitor, www.csmonitor.com; p. 25 "Sharzad," interviewed by Human Rights Watch, "The Human Cost: The Consequences of Insurgent Attacks in Afghanistan," 2007, www.hrw.org, p. 31 President Barack Obama, addressing the nation, East Room, Washington DC, May 2, 2011, https://obamawhitehouse.archives.gov/blog/2011/05/02/osama-bin-laden-dead; p. 37 Captain Jason Pak, filmed for "Oral Histories" by the American Veterans Center, www.americanveteranscenter.org, p. 41 Freshta, interviewed by Amnesty International, "'My Children Will Die this Winter,' Afghanistan's Broken Promise to the Displaced," May 31, 2016, www.amnesty.org.